WOMEN
IN HISTORY

WOMEN AND SPORT

Anne Coates

Wayland

WOMEN
IN HISTORY

Series editor: Catherine Ellis
Book editors: Amanda Earl and Jannet King
Consultant: Professor Deirdre Beddoe BA, PhD,
Dip Ed, Reader in History at the Polytechnic of Wales
Designer: Joyce Chester

Front cover: Amateur Athletics Association Championships at Stamford Bridge, Chelsea in July 1928.
Back cover: Top left – Dorothy Odam, at the Civil Service Sports Ground in Chiswick, London, June 1939. Top right – British tennis player, Charlotte Sterry at Wimbledon in 1908. Bottom left – Olympic medallist Fatima Whitbread. Bottom right – Geraldine Rees, the first woman ever to finish the Grand National.

First published in 1989 by
Wayland (Publishers) Limited
61 Western Road, Hove
East Sussex, BN3 1JD, England

© Copyright 1989 Wayland (Publishers) Limited

British Library Cataloguing in Publication Data
Coates Anne
    Women in sport. (Women in history)
    1. Sports. Role of women
    I. Title II. Series
    796'.01'94

ISBN 1–85210–392–2

Typeset by Kalligraphics Limited, Horley, Surrey
Printed in Italy by G. Canale & C.S.p.A., Turin
Bound in the UK by Mac Lehose & Partners, Portsmouth

Picture acknowledgements
Allsport: back cover, bottom left (Steve Powell), 13, 14, 16 (top), 26, 29, 32, (top), 34 (Tony Diffey), 36 (top) (John Gichigi), 38 (Steve Powell), 39 (Trevor Jones), 40 (top) (David Conner); The Ancient Art and Architecture Collection 4 (top); Barnaby's Picture Library 33, 36 (bottom); Colorsport 37, 42 (top and bottom); Mary Evans Picture Library 6 (top), 8, 10, 11 (left and right), Phil Holden 44; Hulton Picture Company: back cover, top right, 4 (bottom), 5, 7, (top and bottom), 9 (right), 20; Eileen Langsley 43 (top); Billie Love 17; Macdonald/Aldus Archive 9 (left), 15, 25 (bottom left), Oxford Mail and Times 35 (right); Popperfoto 12, 16 (bottom), 19 (top and bottom), 23, 25 (top), 25 (bottom right), 31; Salisbury Times 35 (left); Sport and General 27; Topham: back cover, top left and bottom right, 18, 22, 28; John Warburton 24. The artwork on page 12 is by Thames Cartographic Services.

Contents

Above: *A Greek statuette of a Spartan female athlete, 530 BC.*

Below: *The sporting prowess of fifteenth-century women archers must have been hindered by their long dresses and flowing trains.*

Introduction

As long ago as 1000 BC the women worshippers of the goddess Hera were competing in their own female-only games, and it is most likely that the ancient Greek Olympic Games were based on these. However, since those ancient times women have had a hard struggle to compete in a field which is thought of as primarily male.

Over the centuries, upper-class and aristocratic women – baronesses, duchesses and princesses – have traditionally enjoyed riding, hunting and tennis, while poorer women have been confined to the home or workplace. There is an account from 1591 of Queen Elizabeth I shooting deer with a crossbow

Left: *The few women who did manage to break out of the traditional Victorian female role and take part in dangerous and strenuous sports were hampered by having to wear conventional clothes. This female mountaineer conformed by wearing a fashionable hat and full-length costume with a bustle.*

and, some nine years later, it was noted that women at her court who took part in sport had an easier time in childbirth than women who were not physically active. Just over a century later Queen Anne, who was an excellent horsewoman, started official racing for money in 1714.

However, in general, sport was not a part of ordinary women's lives. If sport figured in their lives at all, they were spectators rather than participants. This is still true of many women today who 'support' male sports at a local level by providing teas after matches and washing the team's kit afterwards. Whatever a man's social class, sport of some description is usually a part of his life – even if it only involves watching snooker on the television. Women who get married and have a family, on the other hand, have to make time if they want to continue a favourite sport, and they have to juggle this with family commitments and work.

6

Sport? I'd never have the energy – it takes me all I've got to do the house, look after the kids and go to work – the only thing I like to do in the evenings is sleep or watch a video. Quote from a woman in her late twenties, with three children, and a job as an office worker, 1986. From *All Work and no Play*.

9

Right: *Although frowned upon by men, women did take up sports which were traditionally regarded as male. This group of female footballers formed the Ladies 'South' Team in 1895.*

Below: *Sue Brown, an Oxford chemistry student, made history in 1981 by becoming the first woman cox to take part in the Oxford and Cambridge Boat Race. She retained her seat the following year.*

Girls and women have to be even more dedicated than their male counterparts if they are to succeed in a field that is still, to a large extent, dominated by men. In the past, men have jealously guarded their sports, making women feel that anything which involved them getting sweaty, dirty or building up their muscles would be unladylike and unattractive. Some sports, such as swimming and skating, which allow women to appear graceful, were more acceptable than sports such as athletics, which intruded on the male preserve.

Over the last hundred and fifty years, as women have striven to assert themselves, fighting for the vote, independence and equal rights, men have begun taking sportswomen more seriously, although there is still a long way to go before they are regarded as equals!

This book is about women who have played a part in making sport what it is today. Not everyone or every sport can be included. Those that are, are representative of all those who have taken part in the struggle, often for very little reward. The story of women in sport is one of bravery, daring, dedication and commitment, from the first all-female cricket match in 1835 to women running the 10,000 metres race, introduced at the 1988 Olympic Games in Seoul, Korea. It becomes even more exciting as women continually push back the barriers and compete in sports such as snooker and motor racing, two of the last bastions of 'male' sport.

1

Cricketers and Cyclists

1840–1900

Part of a drawing by George du Maurier of a women's cricket match in 1880.

The Victorian woman was seen first and foremost as a wife and a mother. Regarded as the weaker sex, middle-class women were put on a pedestal, which successfully isolated them from the male world of commerce, politics, the arts and sport. Large families, made popular by Queen Victoria (1819–1901), effectively tied women to the home. Upper- and middle-class ladies' leisure time was spent paying calls, embroidering and perhaps riding or playing a gentle game of tennis, whereas lower-class women had little if any time to call their own. Those who worked, usually in domestic service or in sweatshops, toiled long hours for very little pay, and then mothers and daughters alike had to go home to see to the family's needs.

In 1792 Mary Wollstonecraft in *Vindication of the Rights of Woman* had advocated exercise as a way to make women look more healthy, suggesting that it would make them think independently as well – not something most men of the day wanted to encourage! But although working-class women began to unite

6
While enervated [weakened] by confinement and false notions of modesty, the [female] body is prevented from attaining that grace and beauty which relaxed half-formed limbs never exhibit.
Mary Wollstonecraft *Vindication of the Rights of Woman*, 1792.
9

Left: *Women cricketers in the 1880s took their sport very seriously, although they must have been encumbered by their long, heavy skirts.*

A few hats went flying in the rough and tumble of hockey matches. Everyday dresses had to be worn, in order to respect the conventions of the day.

in unions from the 1840s onwards, and both working- and middle-class women fought for the right to vote, there was no group to fight for the rights of women in sport. In fact, politically active women virtually ignored this area of female emancipation. Medical opinion was against sport for women. It was thought that women only had a certain amount of energy and any expended on sport would mean less for producing children.

Undeterred, some women were joining forces and taking sport into their own hands. In 1886, the 'Original English Lady Cricketers', two professional teams accompanied by a manager and a chaperone, toured the country playing exhibition matches. The following year the first women's hockey club was founded.

Women played tennis socially, but were not allowed into the All England Croquet and Lawn Tennis Club until 1884. That year, Maud Watson beat her elder sister Lilian in the first ever ladies' singles final. Four years later no one expected young Charlotte 'Lottie' Dod, the ladies' singles champion, to defeat Wimbledon champion Ernest Renshaw in a handicapped exhibition match.

It was not just that women were supposedly weaker than men, they were also greatly disadvantaged by the clothes they wore. Women taking part in sport dressed conventionally, in clothes similar to their everyday outfits, in order to preserve their respectability. They were hampered by long skirts and uncomfortable, tight whalebone corsets that rubbed under the arms so much that they often caused blisters and bleeding after a match. It was not long before clothing manufacturers saw the potential for specifically designed women's sportswear, but although slightly looser and less fussy than before, the outfits were still very restrictive and completely covered the body. There was hardly any difference in dress between the women participating in sport and those spectating.

Lack of suitable attire did not put women off the new craze for bicycling, although those who adopted the fashion for 'bloomers' – long, loose baggy culotte-type trousers gathered at the knee – did gain more freedom of movement.

The first bike for women, designed in 1874, had a side-saddle. It was not until 1887 that the crossbar on a bike was bent to make it more suitable for women riders, and within a few years women made up 50 per cent of cyclists. Some took their sport

Below left: *A fashionable tennis outfit from 1900. In fact it differed little from the clothes worn every day.*

Below right: *Women were very keen to take up cycling in the late nineteenth century, and some were glad to give up their voluminous dresses in favour of the new fashion of wearing bloomers.*

First, three young Englishmen, all strong-armed and accomplished bicyclers, held the machine in place while I climbed timidly into the saddle. Frances E. Willard, *A Wheel Within a Wheel*, 1895.

Below: *Early gymnastic exercises for girls bear little resemblance to the skill and technical brilliance we associate with the sport today, but their introduction marked a major step forward for sportswomen.*

very seriously indeed. At the turn of the century, Mrs Ward, still hampered by her long dress, made the 190 kilometre London–Brighton–London round trip in six and a half hours. Maggie Foster managed to reduce the time by one hour when she undertook the journey going in the opposite direction, with a motorcycle to pace her. An astonishing 480 kilometres were clocked up by Kate Green of York in her 24-hour cycling expedition. Nowadays the annual journey from London to Brighton is completed as a 'fun run' and times are not registered, but even with their lightweight bicycles and other modern equipment, most cyclists today would find it hard to beat those times.

In the 1870s, another sport began to take hold in schools – Per Henrik Ling's Swedish gymnastics. These were gentle exercises designed for girls, and in 1878 the London School Board appointed Madame Bergman-Osterberg as teacher of gymnastics in elementary schools. Forty of her pupils appeared in the May/June International Health Exhibition. They won a gold

medal for their performance. Madame Osterberg also started a college to train gym teachers. This opened up a new career for women and as there was no comparable college for male physical education teachers until 1930, it was an area in which women took the lead.

At public schools for girls, including Roedean in Sussex and Cheltenham Ladies College, team games were encouraged. Sports like lacrosse and netball were acceptable because, being all-women sports, they did not represent a challenge to male supremacy.

Your girls play [cricket] like gentlemen and behave like ladies. J. F. Dove *Work and Play in Girls' Schools*, 1891.

Charlotte Dod (1871–1960)

Charlotte 'Lottie' Dod was tennis's first child prodigy and the first real athlete of the game. She was born in Cheshire and began playing tennis with her sister and two brothers. When she was only eleven years old she won her first major title, the ladies' doubles at the 1882 Northern Tournament in Manchester, partnering her nineteen-year-old sister, Ann.

By the age of twelve she was known as 'the little wonder' and her early potential was proved when she won the Wimbledon Championship at fifteen years old. In over one hundred years of the Wimbledon Championship she has remained the youngest ever champion. Her youth gave her one advantage – she was allowed to play in a shorter skirt than the older women, giving her more leeway to jump and run. Her game was full of exuberance, and her co-ordination, speed, physical strength and competitive spirit made her more like the male players of the time.

Lottie's exhibition handicapped match against Ernest Renshaw, the current men's champion, was an amazing feat and she went on to repeat the performance when she defeated William Renshaw, with six Wimbledon titles to his credit, later the same year. Clearly she had disproved the idea that the sport was too physically taxing for women!

Lottie went on to win Wimbledon four more times and when she felt the challenge was not enough she transferred her talents to another sport – golf. She won the Ladies' Open Golf Championship at Troon in Scotland in 1904. Skating also took her fancy, but not content with just the women's tests of expertise, she passed those for men as well. Stretching her sporting skills still further, she played hockey at international level and took the silver medal for archery in the 1908 Olympic Games at the age of thirty-seven.

Above: *A portrait of Charlotte Dod.* **Right:** *The match between Ernest Renshaw and Lottie Dod.*

E. Renshaw.

Miss L. Dod,
Winner of the Ladies Championship.

When women took over what were traditionally male jobs during the First World War, they also adopted men's clothes for working.

2

The Modern Olympics

1900–1914

The beginning of the twentieth century marked a turning point for sportswomen. In the first modern Olympic Games of 1896, no women were allowed to take part. Four years later, however, 12 were allowed to compete (as opposed to 1,318 men). British tennis player Charlotte Sterry, three-times winner of the ladies' singles at Wimbledon, became the first female Olympic champion in any sport.

Two years later a very determined Madge Syers was placed second in the World Figure Skating Championship. She had taken part in a competition that was supposed to be only for men, so her success must have been a double blow to the other competitors. When skating was included in the Olympic Games six years later, Madge became the first female champion.

In fact, the 1908 Olympic Games, which were held in London,

> **Women have but one task, that of crowning the winner with garlands.** Baron Pierre de Coubertin, initiator of modern Olympic Games, 1902.

Comparison of numbers of men and women competing in the modern Olympic Games. Both the total number of competitors and the proportion of women to men have increased steadily.

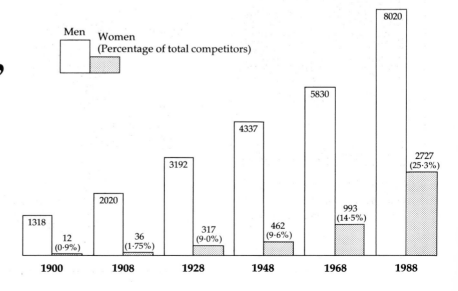

Men
Women
(Percentage of total competitors)

1900	1908	1928	1948	1968	1988
1318	2020	3192	4337	5830	8020
12 (0·9%)	36 (1·75%)	317 (9·0%)	462 (9·6%)	993 (14·5%)	2727 (25·3%)

showed an increase in female participation. There were still only 36 women competitors (compared with 2,020 men), but this was a great improvement on the previous Olympic Games, when there had only been eight women taking part. British women made their presence felt. Along with Madge Syers' gold for figure skating, Queenie Newell won the gold medal for archery while Lottie Dod took the silver. Another Briton, Frances Clytie Rivett-Carnac, became the first woman to win an event not restricted to women, when she and her husband won the 7-metre class yachting. Women have crewed such races ever since.

By the time of the next Olympics, held in Stockholm, Sweden, the percentage of women taking part had fallen again. Only 55 women participated in a field of 2,546 athletes, a ratio of one woman to every 56 men! Except in the case of mixed doubles at tennis, women competed only against each other. Swimming and highboard diving had joined tennis, archery, figure skating and yachting as sports suitable for women to compete in. Golf had been included in the 1904 Games, but was discontinued for both men and women and has yet to be reinstated. Archery suffered a similar fate after Queenie Newell's victory in 1908, but was brought back into the games in 1972.

Before the First World War (1914–1918), which was to change people's lives irrevocably, early twentieth-century women were

At the Olympic Games in London in 1908, women gymnasts gave demonstrations of their skill, although they were not allowed to compete until the 1928 Games.

‘ *…excessive devotion to athletics and gymnastics tends to produce what may perhaps be called the 'neuter' type of girl. Her figure instead of developing to full female grace, remains childish… she is flat-chested with a badly developed bust, her hips are narrow and in too many instances there is a corresponding failure to function.* Dr Mary Scharlieb, *Recreational Activities of Girls during Adolescence*, 1911. ’

Right: *A line-up of Britain's swimming team who competed in the 4 × 100 metres relay in the 1912 Stockholm Olympics.*

still impeded by their clothing. Skirts were worn ankle-length, even for such sports as skiing, ice-skating, hiking, mountain climbing and horse riding. As the idea of specifically designed sportswear caught on, so clothes and outfits for all sorts of sports became an essential part of every society lady's wardrobe. The idea of dressing the part was frequently more appealing than actually taking part. Similarly, in the 1980s fashion conscious girls and women took to wearing leg-warmers, sweat bands and designer tracksuits, even if they never went near a gym or exercise studio.

During the First World War, women were suddenly freed both physically and mentally from the many conventions that had restricted their lifestyles. When the men went off to war, women took over many 'male' occupations – on the buses and trams, in engineering and in offices. They also did war work – in munitions factories and in agriculture. Trousers became a more acceptable form of dress for those in the Women's Land Army, who worked in the fields growing crops, although they were still not really regarded as 'respectable' clothing for women outside working hours! However, such moves towards liberation were a major turning point for women, who for the first time could prove that they were just as good as men in many fields – from engineering to sport.

Charlotte Sterry (1871–1966)

One of the most popular players of her day, Charlotte 'Chattie' Cooper was born in Ealing, London, learned to play tennis at the Ealing Lawn Tennis Club and lived within cycling distance of Wimbledon. She won her first open singles title at Ilkley in 1893 and two years later she became both the Irish champion and the Wimbledon ladies' singles champion.

A leader in the field of those early days of women's competitive tennis, Chattie had great stamina (rare in a woman of her time) and played an unusual attacking game. That, and her robust constitution, helped her win both singles and doubles titles all over the country. She took the Wimbledon singles title again in 1896, 1898 and in 1901, the year of her marriage to solicitor Alfred Sterry.

At the first Olympic Games in which women were allowed to compete, in Paris in 1900, Chattie made history by becoming the very first woman in any sport to win an Olympic gold. She defeated Hélène Prevost, the French champion, in the lawn tennis tournament 6–1, 6–4. The two women faced each other across the nets once more in the mixed doubles. Hélène and her partner H.S. Mahony lost to Chattie, who had teamed up with R.F. Doherty.

In 1908 Chattie took all three Wimbledon titles, defeating Mrs Lambert Chambers in the singles and winning the mixed doubles with S.E. Casdagli and the ladies' doubles title with Miss Garfit. Some eighteen years after her first Wimbledon victory, Chattie, aged forty-two, again reached the finals of the ladies' doubles. She retired from the game that year, leaving behind her a powerful example for other women players to emulate. Her sportsmanship and good temper, coupled with her supreme steadiness and great tactical ability made her the object of admiration and respect.

> *A quite unusually strong and active girl, with a constitution like the proverbial ostrich, who scarcely knew what it was like to be tired, and was never sick or sorry. She once told me she had heard of such things but did not know what a headache was.* Commander George Hillyard, a contemporary, cited in *Faster, Higher, Further* by Adrianne Blue.

Respected and admired for her good nature and sportmanship, Charlotte Sterry was a trail-blazer in women's tennis.

3

Between the Wars

1918–1939

Sonja Henie of Norway, three times Olympic gold medallist.
Below: *Suzanne Lenglen shocked Wimbledon with her revealing clothes, but she played exciting tennis.*

After the First World War, women were encouraged to return to their 'natural' functions of childbearing, motherhood and looking after men. However, the liberating experiences of working in interesting, although tiring, jobs had altered women's views. One woman summed it up by saying, 'women never went back to the fireside in the same way after the war'.

Wimbledon tennis was taken by storm in 1919 by French woman Suzanne Lenglen, who shocked everyone by daring to shorten her skirt and stop wearing her corset. This was not just a fashion whim. It was done with the primary intention of improving her game. Instead of playing from the base line as women had traditionally done, she ran to the net and so began

the slow, but steady, transformation of women's tennis from a nice sedate game played in long skirts and bustles to the cut and thrust power game it is today.

Suzanne Lenglen was effectively sport's first female superstar. She drank, smoked and courted the media. Her 'aggressive' play was tolerated because she was also glamorous and feminine. Wimbledon women continued to lead the field in sportswear, with the first appearance of short trousers in 1931. 'Bobby sox' also began to replace stockings.

Fashion wasn't such a problem for swimmers, however. Belle White had been Britain's first medallist in plain high-diving, with her Stockholm bronze in 1912. She went on to win 25 gold medals for plain diving in England between 1912 and 1929 and, proving that age was no barrier, competed in the first European Games in Bologna in 1927, when she was thirty-three.

In another traditionally acceptable women's sport, figure skating, Norwegian Sonja Henie, who later became extremely wealthy from her appearances in films and ice shows, introduced jumps into her repertoire and won the gold in three successive Games: 1928, 1932 and 1936.

While diving and figure skating were firmly established as women's events in the Olympics, track and field events were still restricted to men only. The strength and stamina needed were regarded as masculine qualities. Not to be beaten, the Federation Sportive Feminine Internationale (the international women's sporting union) was founded in 1921 and decided to put on its own athletics competition that year. At the first games

> **❛** *...In 1930, 33 year-old Marjorie Foster beat 99 soldiers, sailors and airmen to win shooting's King's Prize, the Championship of the British Empire at Bisley, near London. She told Lord Jellicoe: 'I was just treating this as a pleasant afternoon's shooting.'* From Sheila Fletcher, *Women First.* **❜**

Left: *Mary Lines was first past the post in the 250 metres staged by the international women's sporting union in 1921 in France.*

in Monte Carlo 100 women took part. The next year 300 women competed. It took until 1928 for women track and field competitors to be admitted to the official Olympic Games. Events, however, were limited to the 100 metres and the 100 metres relay, high jump and discus. The javelin and the 80 metres hurdles were added in 1932, when both gold medals (the hurdles being decided with the use of a new technique, the photo-finish) were won by American Mildred 'Babe' Didrikson. Born into a large, poor Norwegian family which had emigrated to the USA, Babe became the darling of America. She excelled at everything she tackled and in that same Olympics also won the silver medal for high jump.

One event which had been included in the 1928 Games was the 800 metres, in spite of the fact that it was considered too arduous a race for women. In fact the first three women to

Below: *Mildred Didrikson, USA, (right of picture) competing in the 80 metres hurdles in the 1932 Los Angeles Olympics. She set a world record for this event and also won the gold for javelin.*

Left: *Lina Radke of Germany won the 800 metres in the 1928 Amsterdam Olympics, beating Japan's Kinuye Hitomi by less than a second.*

‘

Runner Harold Abrahams' commented on the women's 800 metres controversy of 1928: **The 800 metres was a scene of very limited amount of distress among the defeated [women] competitors, and somewhat sensational writing by many of the journalists present resulted in that event being omitted [from future games].**

’

reach the post had all bettered the women's world record, but some runners, unused to the distance and having had little opportunity to run it before, collapsed from exhaustion. The race was then removed for women on the grounds that it was unsuitable, and was not returned to the Olympic Games until thirty-six years later.

Unfortunately, that race added fuel to the notion that women were the 'weaker sex' – a belief that was further encouraged by the newspapers. Two years earlier, on 6 August 1926, the

Entering the Channel before her arduous swim, Gertrude Ederle was to make history as the first woman to complete the crossing.

very day that New Yorker Gertrude Ederle became the first woman to swim the English Channel faster than any man, these words appeared in the *London Daily News*: 'Even the most uncompromising champion of the rights and capabilities of women must admit that in contests of physical skill, speed and endurance they must remain forever the weaker sex.' A year later Ivy Gill became the first Englishwoman to complete the channel crossing, doing so at the latest ever date in the year, 14 October.

Women competing in events or areas that involved a long distance became taboo. Marathon running was completely out of the question, so Violet Piercy ran the distance unofficially. She completed the London circuit in 3 hours 40 minutes, 22 seconds on 3 October, 1926. Her record remained until 1963, when American Mary Lepper cut 3 minutes 22 seconds off the time. The following year Dale Greig an Englishwoman, broke the psychological barrier of 3 hours 30 minutes, running unofficially in a marathon on the Isle of Wight and finishing in 3 hours 27 minutes, 45 seconds.

Involving themselves in competitive sport was an uphill struggle for women, but through it all women's groups organized themselves and pressed ahead. Women's team games flourished. There were international tours for female cricketers, hockey, lacrosse and netball players, but as these had to be funded by the players themselves (this is still the case today for the England women cricketers) it meant the sports were only open to women who could afford the fares. The year 1935, however, saw some moves forward, with the foundation of the United Women's Team Games Board. Also, in the following year a grant of £100 was given by the National Fitness Council so that an office could be set up and a national organizer employed to promote team games for women in England and Wales.

Lack of money was a definite drawback for some sportswomen, but others were still effectively barred from sports because of childbearing. In 1921, Marie Stopes opened the first British birth control clinic and by 1930 local authorities were allowed to provide limited birth control advice. Contraception gave women a much greater control over their physical lives. Being able to limit the size of their families and delay having babies led to greater freedom for women to pursue their own interests, including sport.

However, the start of the Second World War (1939–45) meant that once again women had to fill the jobs left vacant by men going off to fight.

4

Post-war Recognition

1945–1960

Fanny Blankers-Koen (left), winner of the 100 metres hurdles at the 1948 London Olympics, being congratulated by the runner-up, Maureen Gardner.

When the Second World War ended and peace returned women were once again actively urged to adopt the roles of wives, mothers and homemakers. To some extent this was encouraged because of the government's worry over the falling population figures. Women who worked – and they were mainly unmarried – did gain equal pay in teaching and the civil service, but the stereotype was of a woman staying at home to look after her husband and children, a role heavily reinforced by the media.

Some women, however, proved that being a mother and a sportswoman was not incompatible. Many women athletes had been left 'on ice' during the war and were therefore older than usual when they next competed at the 1948 Olympics held in London. Fanny Blankers-Koen beat British competitor Maureen Gardner in the 100 metres hurdles race in spite of being eleven years older and the mother of two children.

'━━━━━━━━

Fastest Woman in the World is an Expert Cook' Headline describing Fanny Blankers-Koen, *Daily Graphic* 5 August, 1948.

━━━━━━━━**,**

Left: *Taking the second hurdle in their stride (from right to left), the winner Fanny Blankers-Koen (Holland), Maureen Gardner (GB) who finished second, Maria Oberbreyer (Austria), Y. Monginue (France) and Shirley Strickland (Australia) who came in third in the 80 metres hurdles at the 1948 London Olympics.*

Pat Smythe riding Flanagan during the Equestrian Olympics Grand Prix jumping event in Stockholm 1956. The British team won the bronze medal.

Other women whose sporting careers managed to span the war included ice skater Cecilia Colledge, who held the British title from 1935 to 1938 and again in 1946, and Isobel Roe, who was the British ladies' ski-running champion in 1938 and 1939 and again in 1948 and 1949.

Television made a great impact on sport (although by no means every home had one). It made sport more accessible to spectators, and gave sportsmen and women a higher profile and greater recognition than ever before. Nowadays huge fees are paid to broadcast major sporting events, but back in 1957 when the first netball matches were played at the Empire Pool, Wembley, the main match, England versus The Rest, was televised for a fee of just ten guineas!

The following year, with major changes in the rules, a new netball rule book was published. A record 53,500 copies were sold in one year, with England captain Jo Higgins personally handling the sale and despatch of 35,000 copies before arrangements were made for the printer to take over distribution.

In the equestrian field, record-breaker Pat Smythe won the British Show Jumping Association's Ladies' Championship in 1952, 1953, 1955, 1957–9 and 1961–2. Although horseriding has always been an acceptable sport for upper-class women, the Olympics were slow to admit women riders. Showjumping, dressage and three-day-eventing were restricted to men only until 1952, when the first four women were allowed to compete, against men, in dressage. One of them, Lis Hartel from Denmark, won the silver medal. Four years later a female show-jumper shared her team's bronze medal. Women have steadily infiltrated the field ever since, so that by 1984 one third of the three-day-eventers were female.

In spite of the fact that gymnastics had begun as a female sport, it took a long time for women to be able to compete on an individual basis. Men's gymnastics had been included in the first modern Olympics and it had been introduced as a team event for women in 1928. The first medals for individual women gymnasts were awarded in 1952, when women from behind the Iron Curtain led the field and have continued to do so.

In the same year, at the Winter Olympics, Jeanette Altwegg won a gold medal for figure skating. Later she was to give up her career as a skater to work with orphan children at a Pestalozzi Village in Switzerland.

During the post-war years fashion on the tennis courts took an upward leap, with skirts becoming extremely short. British tennis star 'Gorgeous Gussy' Moran made this new fashion her trademark and later sported leopardskin shorts for a professional game at Madison Square Garden. Such sportswear was both practical and emphasized the femininity of the players, but comment was starting to focus on what the players were wearing, rather than on how well they were playing.

In the less glamorous world of table tennis, between 1950 and 1965, Diane Rowe won the English Open Championship women's doubles twelve times with four different partners. She also won the mixed doubles four times between 1952 and 1969.

The post-war period was a great time for roller skating, always a popular sport in the streets. Lesley Woodey from Birmingham won twelve British national individual speed titles over three regulation distances of 804 metres, 1.6 kilometres and 8 kilometres between 1957 and 1964. Then Londoner Chloe Ronaldson, between 1958 and 1974, set a record in taking nineteen women's titles.

Below: *Britain's Jeanette Altwegg during a training session for the 1952 Olympics, in which she won the gold for figure skating.*

Jo Higgins (b. 1931)

Josephine Higgins was born in London, the youngest of ten children. Her parents had not participated in any sports at a competitive level, but although they may not have actively encouraged the young Jo to play netball, they did nothing to stop her. Her father had died by the time she began playing for Camberwell's Mary Datchelor Grammar School, which she attended from the age of sixteen to eighteen. Her association with the school continued after she had left, when she played for their 'old girls' team.

Jo went on to teacher training college in Lincoln where she specialized in physical education. She played netball for the college team and was also selected for Lincolnshire county. Her county career continued when, after finishing college, she moved back south and was chosen to play for Surrey and then, in the mid-1950s, she was selected for the England team.

Jo played, on average, two matches a week, one for the club and one for the county side, and there was a practice session once a month for the county team. This was as well as her commitments as a teacher, with the after-school activities that this involved. But Jo's philosophy was that if you are really interested in something, you find the time for it.

Joining the England team meant extra expenses too. Jo was earning £26 a month when she first started teaching, and not much more than that when she had to find £212 to go to South Africa with the team in 1956. She had to try and save as much as she could. By getting an earlier train to work, before 6.20am, she saved 3d a day! She also taught evening classes at the

Jo Higgins captained the English netball team from 1958–60. It was hard for her to find the time and money, but she was prepared to make sacrifices to take part in her chosen sport.

school. The team raised money by playing exhibition matches, and was rewarded by winning every match except one on that first African tour.

Jo captained the England team from 1958 to 1960, and again in 1963 when she played in the first world tournament. She gave up playing in 1966.

Jo went on to coach her county team and then served as secretary on the rules committee. At Mary Datchelor they were taught that if you got something out of a game, you had a responsibility to give something back – which is exactly what Jo Higgins and many women like her have done.

5

Role Models and Superstars

1960–1970

By the 1960s, women were beginning to have a higher profile in most areas of life – and sport was no exception. The majority of families had televisions, and sports coverage was a major part of the television companies' programming. In schools, sports facilities were greatly improved and the subject was taken more seriously, thereby giving more girls the opportunity to discover their athletic potential.

Not only were girls given a wider range of sports to participate in, there were more highly successful woman athletes for them to model themselves on. In the sixties female athletes became headline news. The sprinter Lillian Board MBE, who was among this group of high-profile athletes, was sadly missed when she died tragically young of cancer in 1970. Dorothy Hyam MBE became the first female athlete in Britain to win three medals.

Mary Peters, a sporting star of the sixties and seventies, receiving her gold medal for the Pentathlon at the Munich Olympics in 1972.

Far left: *Lillian Board in May 1970, only months before her tragically early death.*

Left: *A boxer's victory salute from Mary Rand in Tokyo 1964, after she became the first British woman to win an Olympic gold for a track or field event. To her left is silver medallist I. Kirzenstein (Poland) and to her right T. Shelankova (USSR), who won the bronze.*

In the 1960 Olympic Games she won a silver for the 100 metres and a bronze for the 200 metres. Her participation in the 1964 4 × 100 metres relay earned her the bronze.

Team-mate Mary Rand was the first British woman to win an Olympic gold in athletics and she proved that marriage and motherhood were no bar to success. Her daughter was only a few months old when Mary neared the peak of her form. She shared the world relay record in 1963 and in the Tokyo Olympics of 1964 she made the greatest series of long jumps on record, including the world record jump of 6.76 metres which won her the gold. That same Games she won the silver for the pentathlon and the bronze as a member of the British team in the 4 × 100 metres relay. She was created an MBE for her efforts.

Although Mary Rand was below her usual standard, she still won the gold in the Commonwealth Games in 1966. Injury prevented her from taking part in the 1968 Olympics and she retired from competitive athletics.

Below: *Ann Packer winning the 800 metres and a gold for Britain in the Tokyo Olympics, 1964.*

Ann Packer was another golden girl. The defeat of her fiancé, Robbie Brightwell, in the 400 metres race in the Tokyo Olympics in 1964 gave her a new incentive to win a gold. She had won a silver in the women's 400 metres, but as she had not done very well in the heats of the 800 metres had considered dropping out of the event. Then she decided to win the gold for Robbie, and unexpectedly ran a record-breaking race. It was a truly romantic gesture – with the normal roles reversed. The media loved it and, as was the case with every one of this group of female athletes, media exposure showed the public that sport did not take away women's 'femininity', as was once believed during the Victorian and Edwardian period.

1966 was a historic year for the All England Women's Lacrosse Association. Although the Association had been founded as early as 1912, it had to wait until 1966 before appointing an Organizing Secretary, their first full-time paid official. Two years before, when the US team toured Britain, BBC 2 had featured

Below: *England versus the United States in London, 1964. In spite of the fact that they are given little publicity by the media, team games like lacrosse have fared well in Britain, due to the dedication of the players.*

Beryl Burton in action during the World Cycling Championships in Holland, 1967, when she won the bronze in the women's 3000 metres pursuit event.

❝
Frequently track and field events are relegated to the realm of sweat and muscles, unsuitable for the 'gentler sex'. There is nothing wrong with sweat and a strong woman whose figure stands up for itself is made to be admired. John T. Powell, *How to Teach High Jump to Girls*, 1963.
❞

the match against England. This was only the association's second television appearance, the first being in 1951 when it was featured in a BBC Children's Hour.

While some sportswomen were beginning to make an impact, other women behind the scenes still had a tough fight on their hands. The Jockey Club only gave licences to women trainers if they applied in the name of their head stable lads. Florence Nagle took her battle for a licence to court and won in 1966. The Jockey Club now admits women, with some quite spectacular results: Corbière, the winner of the 1983 Grand National, was trained by a woman, Jenny Pitman.

During the 1960s, British amateur cyclist Beryl Burton was at her peak. She held the British Women's Best All-Rounder title every year between 1959 and 1973. She is noted for her achievements in time-trials and up to 1970 she won five gold, three silver and three bronze medals in that event and two golds and one silver in the round race. She was the only woman to beat top-class male riders consistently in open events and obviously impressed her daughter Denise, who followed in her footsteps.

The fact that most sportswomen did not appear tremendously muscle-bound did little to help those women who were more physically developed. Some twenty years later javelin thrower Fatima Whitbread was to say, 'I don't dislike my muscles. I enjoy feeling healthy, looking good,' but during the sixties women who excelled at sport were often regarded as 'not real women', especially if their muscles were well developed. The implication was that if they were that good, they could not really be women!

The culmination of this idea was the institution of sex tests for women in international sport in 1966. Apart from the indignity sportswomen had to suffer, very little thought was given to the shattering effect a failed test would have on a woman's life. The test was used in the 1968 Olympics and Mary Peters, captain of the athletics team, was so concerned about the implications that she arranged with the British organizers for any woman who failed the test to be rushed to an isolation hospital saying she had a mysterious virus. It is unlikely that this would have fooled either the media or a public avid for sensational stories, but in the event the ruse did not have to be used. All the British women passed the test.

In the fashion world, the advent of the mini skirt and tights gave women much greater freedom of movement. This theme was reflected in sports clothes, which became more practical. A much wider range of synthetic fibres was available, giving sports clothes more elasticity and making them less restrictive.

Mary Peters (b. 1939)

Mary Peters represented Northern Ireland at every Commonwealth Games between 1958 and 1974. However, Belfast is only her adopted city. She was born in the outskirts of Liverpool, but moved to Ireland in the 1950s, and has steadfastly remained in Belfast throughout its troubles.

Mary's first real steps on the road to her Olympic and Commonwealth Games successes were taken when a far-sighted teacher allowed her to join the boys for athletics (the girls' class was not so advanced). Almost every Saturday Mary competed at sports meetings all over Northern Ireland, and by the time she was fifteen she was a rising star.

After teaching Domestic Science, Mary went to work full-time for her coach, Buster McShane, at his gym. In 1961 she became a British international, coming fourth in the pentathlon at the 1964 Tokyo Olympics and second in the shot at the 1966 Commonwealth Games in Jamaica. Four years later Mary was well on the way to her Olympic gold, coming first in the shot and pentathlon at the Edinburgh Commonwealth Games.

Throughout her career Mary suffered many disappointments, but winning the gold in the pentathlon at the Munich Olympics in 1972 made up for everything.

At first, it was suggested that Mary's victory should be commemorated by setting up a fund to send women athletes to train in England. Mary was against the idea. She wanted to raise the money to build a track in Belfast so that thousands could enjoy the facilities instead of the few who would benefit from being sent to England.

Mary began working to this end while she trained for the 1974 Christchurch Commonwealth Games where she was to win the pentathlon. Christchurch was Mary's last appearance as an athlete, but since then she has worked tirelessly, raising money for the track which was opened in 1976, and promoting the positive face of Belfast, where ordinary people live and work together and perhaps dream of winning an Olympic gold.

Below: *High jump was just one of the five events in which pentathlete Mary Peters had to compete.*

The Sports Council's campaign, Sport for All, was aimed at getting more people interested in sport. Launched in 1972, it was followed in the 1980s by one which was aimed specifically at women.

> In 1973 Marie McCard pulled a lorry down Bedford High Street using her teeth.
> **'I wanted to prove that it could be done by a woman!'** she said.
> From Sheila Fletcher, *Women First*.

6

Sport for All

1970–1980

The 1970s were a turning-point for women. It was the second wave of the fight for women's liberation, for equal rights. In its own way sport was liberating women and improving the status of racial minorities. Top-class women athletes could earn a good living from sport – though never as much as their male colleagues. Whatever racial prejudices there were (and are) in Britain, white people seemed happy to accept men and women from racial minority groups when they were winning medals. Successful black women athletes provided an excellent role model and inspiration for the next generation.

Participation in sport at any level increases a person's sense of well-being, which is a great psychological plus for women. Exercise is a great antidote to depression. During the 1970s, women began to feel they had more control over their lives their bodies and physical strength. In 1972, the 'Sport For All' campaign was launched by the Sports Council, a government-backed body. 'Sport For All' encouraged everybody, young and old, male and female, to participate more in sport in their local areas. This was followed by their 'Come Alive' campaign in 1977.

The government could also be seen to be taking the issue of women's sport more seriously when they awarded a grant to the All England Lacrosse Association, so that they could appoint a Development Officer in 1970. However, it was only a token award. Britain has never backed its athletes properly with either funds or facilities, and finance has always been a major problem for women competitors, who have lagged far behind men in the sponsorship stakes.

The Sex Discrimination Act of 1975 did very little in real terms to help sportswomen, as sport is excluded under section 44: 'Where the physical strength, stamina or physique of the average woman puts her at a disadvantage to the average man...as a competitor.' In spite of this, women have fought for equality. Twelve-year-old Theresa Bennet sadly lost her court case to keep her place in her local under-twelves football team, even though she had proved herself a tackler to be reckoned with.

Left: *Disabled swimmers taking part in the Para Olympics in Seoul. The first Olympic Games for paraplegics was introduced in 1960.*

Women snooker players also fought to convince courts in Belfast and Sheffield that they had been unlawfully discriminated against by a publican and the YMCA.

Another group which was (and still is) discriminated against was the disabled. The first Paraplegic Olympics (for people with spinal injuries which have led to paralysis) were held in 1960, and they have been going strong ever since, gradually including other people with a wider range of disabilities, such as amputees and the visually handicapped. They are now called the Para (meaning parallel) Olympics. Most disabled athletes, like gold medallist swimmer Monica Vaughan, would prefer their Games incorporated in the able-bodied ones. Realistically they cannot see this happening, but in their Seoul Olympics in 1988, they were given equal status and the British team was allowed to wear the same uniform and athletics clothes as the able-bodied team. Women, however, made up only a quarter of the team.

Right: Olga Korbut (USSR) brought an element of danger and risk into gymnastics when she took the Olympic gold in Munich, 1972.

In the 1972 Munich Olympics there were still nearly six times as many men competing as women. It was the year Mary Peters won her pentathlon gold, and Lorna Johnstone, at the age of seventy, represented Great Britain and was placed twelfth in dressage. At the other end of the age scale, a diminutive Olga Korbut, who appeared much younger than her seventeen years, charmed the spectators with her gymnastics as well as her tears when she made a mistake. Olga, from the Soviet Union, made gymnastics acceptable for women all over the world.

It was rumoured that Olga's trainer had given her drugs to hold back puberty, and much criticism was directed at the intensive coaching given to Eastern bloc athletes and gymnasts. This is not so different, however, from what sometimes happens in Britain, as sprinter Sonia Lannerman found out. She competed in the National junior team and became the European Junior Champion in 1973, but her success in one area was at the expense of another. Because she was good at sports she was encouraged to concentrate on training rather than her school-work. No one considered her long-term future when she would need a job as well.

In 1972 women were finally allowed to race in Great Britain under Jockey Club rules, which meant that women were allowed to ride over jumps in steeplechases. Opportunities are still comparatively few, but there are now approximately 300 women jockeys.

Riding has always been an elitist sport, due to the cost of keeping horses and stabling. It is nevertheless a sport in which women have excelled. The three-day-event is a demanding challenge and one which has been met by Princess Anne, European Champion and Sports Personality of 1971. Lucinda Green (née Prior-Palmer) is the only person to have won both Badminton

Below: *Women jockeys parade their horses in the paddock before the first ladies' race at Kempton Park on May 6, 1972.*

6 ——————
People kept asking me afterwards if I had changed after I won Wimbledon or if winning Wimbledon had changed my life. Really it was because I had managed to change my life that I won.
Virgina Wade, from *Ladies of the Court*.
——————— 9

Right: *Virginia Wade's determination and hard work were finally rewarded when she won the Ladies' Wimbledon title in 1977.*

Horse Trials and Burley in the same season and was awarded the MBE in 1978.

In 1977, Virginia Wade won the ladies' singles tennis at Wimbledon. This was a personal triumph after years of hard work and disappointment. Virginia's win was highly publicized. That was not the case for Karen Taylor who, switching from competing as a swimmer, was the 1979 World Cup winner of the modern pentathlon, which includes riding, fencing, shooting, swimming and running. This event is believed to be one of the greatest physical, as well as psychological, tests of an athlete. Women in sport were finally proving themselves, even though they were not always getting the publicity they deserved.

Monica Vaughan (b. 1952)

Monica Vaughan thinks of herself first and foremost as a swimmer, not as a disabled person, and she only realized that other people regard her as an amputee at the height of her success, when she had just won five gold medals in the 1976 Para Olympics in Toronto. At a reception people kept asking her coach how often she trained, as if she could not answer for herself.

Monica lost a leg in a bus accident when she was four years old. At school, Monica proved she was naturally good at all sports, but swimming gave her the most satisfaction. She regularly competed in swimming events against able-bodied swimmers, and having swum for her city, Portsmouth, she gained the opportunity for a time-trial for her county, Hampshire.

Training three times a day, seven days a week until she left school at eighteen, Monica found she could not combine such commitment with her new career in nursing. Reluctantly she gave up competitive swimming until she heard about sport for amputees in 1975 and joined the team going to the Toronto Para Olympics. There she was the most successful British competitor. In the 1980 Games she retained four of her titles and won another silver medal. In the following two Olympics no one has beaten her records set in the 100 metre butterfly and 100 metre breaststroke for women.

Feeling she was competing just to win medals and no longer prepared to do such heavy training, Monica retired from competitive swimming after the 1980 Olympics, but went on to become the Development Officer for the British Sports Association for the Disabled in 1987. The emphasis in Monica's life has always been on her sport, not her disability. The public should be proud of Monica, as a British gold medallist, but like many others she has never received the full recognition due to her.

Proving that losing a leg need not bar you from taking part in sport, Monica Vaughan's Para Olympic record for the 100 metres butterfly still stands.

Monica Vaughan won five medals in the 1980 Para Olympics, but has received little recognition.

7

Working Out and Olympic Triumphs

The 1980s

Above: *Karen Briggs' technical expertise won her the World Judo Championship.*
Below: *Many women were enticed into gyms and dance studios when exercise classes became fashionable.*

The 1980s saw an explosion of aerobic, body-conditioning and stretch classes, largely thanks to Jane Fonda and her workout books and tapes. Suddenly it became fashionable to be seen to be fit and healthy. Running and jogging were made popular by the famous London Marathon, which brought the sport into the limelight through extensive television coverage and the participation of a large number of celebrities and thousands of ordinary people.

Jogging is easily accessible for most women – because you do not have to spend a lot on special sports clothes and expensive equipment. The one real drawback, made worse in the winter when it gets dark earlier, is the problem of where to run

in safety. However, age and motherhood are no barriers, as forty-four-year-old Joyce Smith, the Commonwealth Marathon record holder proved when she won the women's section of the London Marathon in 1981 and 1982.

Another sport women began to take a greater interest in was judo. It is readily accepted as a 'female sport' as it requires skill and subtlety rather than brute strength. World champion Karen Briggs weighed only 48 kg when she won the title. In the 1988 Olympics judo was included as a demonstration sport for women and table tennis also made its long-awaited debut.

Another sport relatively new to the Olympics is synchronized swimming, which was first included in the 1984 Games. It is an event which has aroused controversy, with some people feeling it is more of an art form, like ballet, and should therefore not be included. In fact, synchronized swimming dates back to

Time and again women have proved that age and motherhood do not impair physical fitness. Joyce Smith was an example to all when she won the women's section of the London Marathon two years in a row.

❛ ──────────

I have eight children, am 72 years old, run every day and I'm a happy woman. Carla Ali, oldest woman marathon runner in 1985.

──────────── **❜**

Right: *Synchronized swimming requires great muscular and breath control – as well as the ability to smile underwater!*

6

This afternoon a girl with a plastic smile and gelatined hair will win the penultimate gold of the Games. It will be awarded for an outstanding performance in holding your breath under water and waggling your legs in the air. David Hun on the introduction of synchronized swimming into the Olympic Games, *Observer* 12 August, 1984.

9

6

They hurt me, but far worse is that they are damaging my sport; and for that I will never forgive them. Sharron Davies talking about the British team officials. Quoted in *Faster, Higher, Further* by Adrianne Blue.

9

the period just after the Second World War, when American swimming champion Ester Williams gave demonstrations of underwater ballet.

Contemporary synchronized swimmers train anything up to twenty hours a week in the water and also practise their 'dry land' routines in a gym. As with skaters, competitors have to perform set figures and three routines. They can take part solo, as a duet or as part of a team of eight. The sport demands just as high a degree of fitness as any other, with some of the participants managing to stay under water for what seems an incredible length of time.

Synchronized swimming is still predominantly a female sport, although there are plans for mixed teams. The inclusion of men is likely to make synchronized swimming, hitherto dismissed as an artform, acceptable as a sport.

Well-known, high-profile sportswomen made huge advances in the eighties, but behind the scenes, from local authorities upwards, most of the officials and coaches are still men. This often creates problems; at a local level male staff trying to encourage more women to take part in sport, forget that a large proportion of women need crèche facilities for their young children. At higher levels, male officialdom still likes to manipulate and control its athletes. This was brought home very firmly to swimmer Sharron Davies, whose method of training before major events differed from that laid down by the British team officials. Sharron was disqualified from the team on a technicality – she had been paid a £40 fee to appear on the television programme *Give Us A Clue*. That, according to the authorities, made her a professional.

Left: *Torvill and Dean introduced a new sensuality into their award-winning ice-dance routines.*

In the year that Tessa Sanderson took the gold medal for javelin throwing and Fatima Whitbread was awarded the bronze, the first women's marathon was included in the 1984 Los Angeles Olympics, and Jayne Torvill, partnered by Christopher Dean, won the gold for ice dancing with the highest-ever score. Some women's events are comparatively new to the games. After Queenie Newell's victory in 1908, archery for women was not included again until 1972. Basketball and rowing made their debut in 1976 and four years later, one hundred years after it was first played by women, hockey was included. Tennis was reinstated as an Olympic sport in 1988 and the women's 10,000 metres was introduced as a track event.

Just under a quarter of the total number of competitors were women in the 1984 Los Angeles Games. This was reflected in the number of women in the British team. For the 1988 Seoul Olympics, Britain fielded a team of 128 women and 233 men.

Right: *Women's hockey made its third Olympic appearance in 1988, with the Australian team taking on Korea in the finals.*

The proportions are becoming more even, but there is still a lot of room for improvement.

One of the reasons why women still play less sport than men is that the people who are in a position to make the decisions in sport are nearly always men. 90 per cent of the recreational managers and national coaches are men, and in schools where there are mixed Physical Education departments 85 per cent are headed by men.

A body which is very much involved in promoting women's interests in sport is the Women's Sports Foundation (WSF). This voluntary organization was set up in 1982 and now has a network of regional offices throughout the country. Its aim is 'to promote the interests of all women in and through sport and to gain equal opportunities and options for women.' The Foundation collects and distributes information about women's sport as well as helping with research projects and ensuring sportswomen are given equal legal rights to men.

One of the concerns of the WSF is the privatization of local authority recreation, such as sports centres. Women's sports and interests, which have taken a long time to be included, will probably be the first to go, if judged on cost effectiveness. One example of this is women-only swimming sessions. They might seem to discriminate against men, but for Muslim women, whose strict religious practices prevent them from exposing their bodies to men other than their husbands, these sessions are their only opportunity to swim.

‘ *When our local sports centre opened I made it my business, as a black woman, to get right in there and make it ours as well.* Denise Hunter. **,**

Fatima Whitbread (b. 1961)

The Fatima Whitbread story is one of determination and dedication. Abandoned as a baby and brought up in a children's home in the East End of London, the young Fatima had a very hard start in life. However, sport, and Margaret Whitbread, her adoptive mother, transformed her life.

Margaret, a former British international javelin thrower herself, taught physical education at the school Fatima attended. She could hardly have been expected to recognize a world-class competitor in the disruptive young girl who joined her classes, but it soon became apparent that Fatima had a natural ability for sport. In coaching Fatima, Margaret gave her the attention the young girl craved and which most children get from their parent or parents.

Fatima was nearly fourteen when she was adopted by Margaret, who became both her mother and coach and gave her the kind of guidance which encouraged competitiveness and a will to succeed.

Dedicated to her sport, Fatima followed a very strict coaching programme, training seven days a week, three or four times a day to build up her muscles. In fact, her height of 163 centimetres meant she was theoretically not tall enough to throw the javelin, but Fatima overcame that drawback, with amazing results. In 1984 she became the Olympic bronze medallist and the following year in Stuttgart she became the first woman in the world to throw a javelin more than 76 metres.

At the 1987 world championships in Rome, Fatima triumphed, beating East German Petra Felke, with whom she shares a friendly rivalry rather different from the

Fatima Whitbread, the 1987 World Champion, is rightly proud of the physique which has made her a world-class javelin thrower.

intense competitiveness between herself and Britain's other world-class javelin thrower, Tessa Sanderson, who took the gold in 1984.

Neither Fatima nor Tessa were at their physical best for the Seoul Olympics in 1988. Tessa did not compete; Fatima struggled to take the silver. It was a bitter disappointment for her, but as someone who has achieved so much in spite of her early disadvantages, it will only be a minor setback in a dazzling career.

8

Sponsorship and the Future

Competent sportswomen like Laura Davies have improved the image of women golfers.

More and more women are now entering areas of sport that were once thought of as primarily for men. Golf was played by women as long ago as the sixteenth century by, amongst others, Mary, Queen of Scots. This century it had a reputation as a sport not played seriously by women. That has all changed with the star appeal of Laura Davies and it is about time there was a women's equivalent of the Ryder Cup.

One reason why there are fewer women athletes is that they find it more difficult to get sponsorship. Fortunately the situation is improving. The NatWest Bank has supported the All England Women's Lacrosse Association and the All England Netball Association, and is one of the many sponsors of the Badminton Association. For individuals the situation is very

Right: *Lucy Soutter in action at the Hi Tec British Open Squash Championships in 1987.*

Left: Sponsorship has made all the difference to the all-England netball team, seen here playing against Trinidad.

different. Allison Fisher, who excels in the very male-dominated world of snooker – she is the Women's UK Champion and World Ladies' Amateur Snooker Champion – is sponsored and managed by Metro Computer Consultants after someone from the company happened to sit next to her father during a tournament! British champion squash player Lucy Soutter has seen her sponsorship grow since her coach sent a written profile of her to various companies. Emily Newman, a winner at Brand's

> **I probably wouldn't be able to do it myself if I wasn't married to a man who is working... he's the coach to the British Olympic dinghy sailing team.**
> Penny Way, champion windsurfer.

Windsurfer Penny Way demonstrating her sport. She admits that she would not be able to compete without her husband's financial support.

Hatch whose racing driving career is really taking off, is sponsored by Pilgrim Air, and windsurfer Penny Way has a grant from the Sports Council as well as sponsorship from a leisurewear company. All these women have one thing in common. They are very determined to compete and have found backers by hook or by crook. The problem for most athletes is that they have to be seen to be winning before anyone will sponsor them, so it can be a vicious circle for women at the beginning of their careers. They have not got the sponsorship to enable them to concentrate on their sport, and without constant training they have little hope of winning.

Women have proved throughout history that they are equal to the challenge of any sport – all they need is for men to give them the opportunity. In fact the idea of the 'weaker sex' is a fallacy. Before puberty, girls are stronger than boys; afterwards the oestrogen levels and fat content rise in preparation for motherhood. In some sports this can be a positive advantage. What is not generally realized is that a woman's muscles are as strong as those of a man who is the same size. Yet women do not, as yet, participate in sports like weight-lifting.

Black sportswoman Molly Samuel is an example to all. Bored with just taking her daughter to and from nursery, she took up karate. The sport opened new prospects for her, and her dedication to fitness and training won her the gold medal at the British Karate Federation National Championships in 1988 and 1989. At twenty-seven she also became the first female coach for the England women's team.

In her book, *Grace Under Pressure*, Adrianne Blue made some perceptive comments about the state of play for women in sport. 'Women are everywhere now,' she wrote. 'The only places they are missing in fair numbers are the sports pages of newspapers and the television screen.' She noted that the BBC's sports round up of 1985 lasted 90 minutes, of which 3 minutes 45 seconds were devoted to women. A similar programme the following year lasted 110 minutes, but only 10 of them were devoted to women. However, in 1988 the Sports Council did launch a million-pound initiative to encourage women to take part in sport. Their aim is to get 1.25 million more women into sport by 1993.

One of the aims of the Women's Sports Foundation is to get the media to give women a fair deal. The way in which women athletes are breaking more and more records, means the media will have to sit up and take note. Sportswomen are and always will be newsworthy.

Projects

Collect all the national newspapers for one week and study them for sports coverage. How many columns are devoted to sportsmen? How much space is allocated to sportswomen? Compare the two figures. Do sportswomen have more coverage in the tabloid press or in the more serious newspapers?

Using your collection of newspapers, compare the language used to describe athletes. Is there any difference in the way sportsmen and sportswomen are described? For example, are women more often described in terms of their physical appearance – 'blonde twenty-two-year-old stunner' – or their other roles, such as 'wife and mother'? In general do you think sportsmen are taken more seriously by the press?

Ask your mother or someone of her age the following questions:

- How much sport did she do at school?
- Did she continue with any of these sports or take up a new sport after leaving school?
- Does she take part in any sport now?

Ask your father or someone of his age the same questions. Compare the answers. What conclusions can you draw?

In class add up the totals for women and men who take part in sport. Then find out the number of girls in the class who think they will continue with sports after they have left school. Do the same for the boys. Compare the two sets of figures. Is there a difference between the two age groups? If so, what do you think the reasons are?

Look for books on sportsmen and sportswomen in your local library, and write down how many men are listed and how many women. If the books are about former athletes, do you think they may have missed out some important sportswomen?

Glossary

Bobby sox Ankle socks.

Corset Women's closely fitting underwear, usually laced tightly at the back and stiffened with whalebone.

Cost effectiveness Making sure something justifies the expense. .

Elitist sport Only accessible to a few, for example those who can afford it.

Emancipation Freeing oneself from legal inequalities and discrimination.

Equestrian field Sports relating to horse-riding events.

Exhibition match A public sports show that is not part of a competition.

Expended Spent, used.

Exuberance High-spiritedness.

Fallacy Delusion, error.

Guineas 21 shillings in pre-decimalized sterling currency.

Handicapped To be given an advantage to compete on equal terms.

Incompatible Not able to exist together in harmony.

Irrevocable Cannot be changed back.

Liberation Freedom.

Muslim A religious follower of Mohammed.

Nazism The policies of the German National Socialist party in Germany in the 1930s and 1940s.

Officialdom The domain or sphere of those holding a position in public office.

Plain diving A term used when 'fancy' diving was introduced in Sweden; a plain dive is a simple forward dive with the body held straight and the arms extended sideways. This is also known as a 'swallow' dive.

Primarily Chiefly.

Privatization The selling off of public assets (ie. those which belong to the country as a whole) to private companies.

Prodigy Someone with exceptional qualities and skills.

Professional A person paid to take part in a sport.

Psychological test Something which tests you mentally.

Representative Typical of a class or group of people.

Status quo An unchanged position or state of affairs.

Books to Read

Allison, M.T., *Women, Work and Leisure: the days of our lives* (Leisure Sciences, 1987).

Blue, Adrianne, *Faster, Higher, Further* (Virago, 1988).

Blue, Adrienne, *Grace Under Pressure* (Sidgwick and Jackson, 1987).

Bowles, S. and Chappell, R., *Women and Athletics* (Athletic Coach, 1986).

Critcher, Charles and Willis, Paul, *Women in Sport* (Centre for Contemporary Cultural Studies, 1974).

Deem, Rosemary, *All Work and No Play* (Oxford University Press, 1986).

Dixey, Rachel, *Asian Women and Sport* (British Journal of Physical Education, 1982).

Duffy, T. and Wade. P., *Winning Women* (Macdonald, 1983).

Dyer, K.F., *Catching up the Men* (Junction Books, 1982).

Ferris, Elizabeth, *Are Women Liberated in Sport?* (Medisport, 1980).

Fletcher, Sheila, *Women First* (Athlone Press, 1984).

Graydon, Jan, *Dispelling the Myth of Female Fragility* (British Journal of Physical Education, 1980).

Kidane, F., *Women in the Olympic Movement* (Continental Sports, 1987).

McCrone, Kathleen, *Sport and the Emancipation of Women 1870–1914* (Routledge, 1988).

Pannick, D., *Sex Discrimination in Sport* (Equal Opportunities Commission, 1983).

Peters, Mary, *Mary P.* (Paul, 1974).

Wade, Virginia and Rafferty, Jean, *Ladies of the Court,* (Pavilion, 1984).

Warrington, Jackie and White, Anita, *Sport and Recreation for Women and Girls* (Sports Council, 1986).

Index

Numbers in **bold** refer to illustrations.